INK
in
INK

BY
JUDI THOMAS

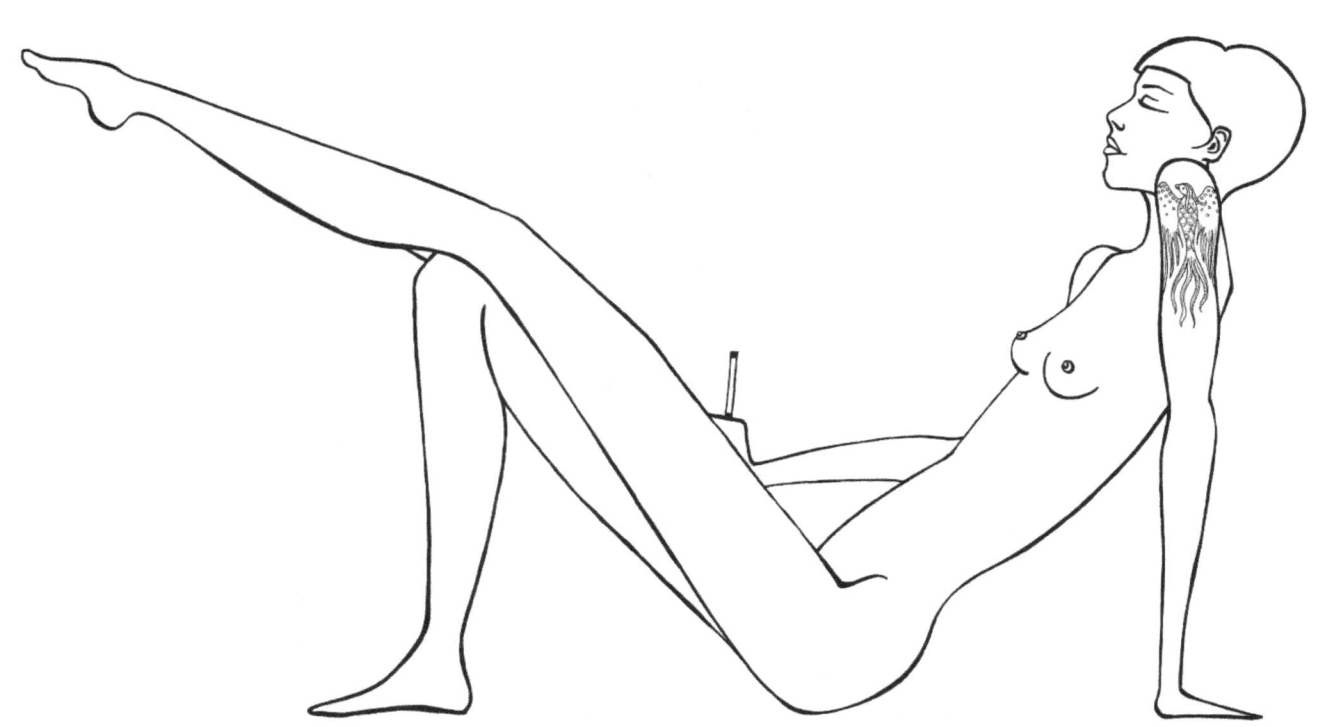

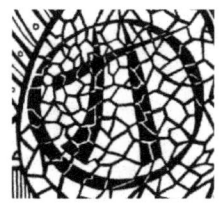

First published 2015 by The Cliterary Press

The Cliterary Press

An imprint of

Judi Thomas Art

www.judithomasart.com

Welcome to INK in INK.
NO RULZ
But here are a few suggestions: You can add
more black lines using a uniPIN fineliner, sizes
3 and 5 are my fav. You can colour using good
quality pencils or felt tips, but remember to
place a sheet of card behind the page you're
working on to protect the picture below. And
when you're done, Tweet or Instagram a photo
of our collaboration #IAmArt @judithomasart

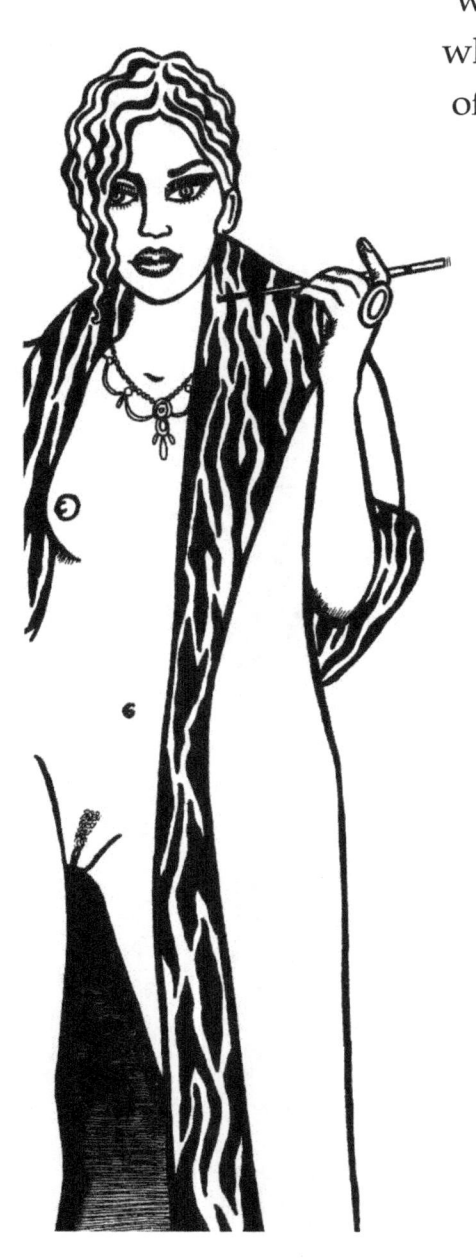

Plate 1   Ms Demeanor

Plate 2   Siren

Plate 3   Cat

Plate 4   Ganesha

Plate 5   Listen

Plate 6   Ms Andry

Plate 7   Ms Behaving

Plate 8   Punk

Plate 9   Tattitude

Plate 10   Miki

Plate 11   Third Eye

Plate 12   Dreaming of Beardsley

Plate 13   Ms Conceived

Plate 14   Ennui

Plate 15   Wrapped up in you

Plate 16   Daydreamer

Plate 18   Booty

Plate 19   Lady Garden

Plate 20   Shell

Plate 1 – Ms Demeanor

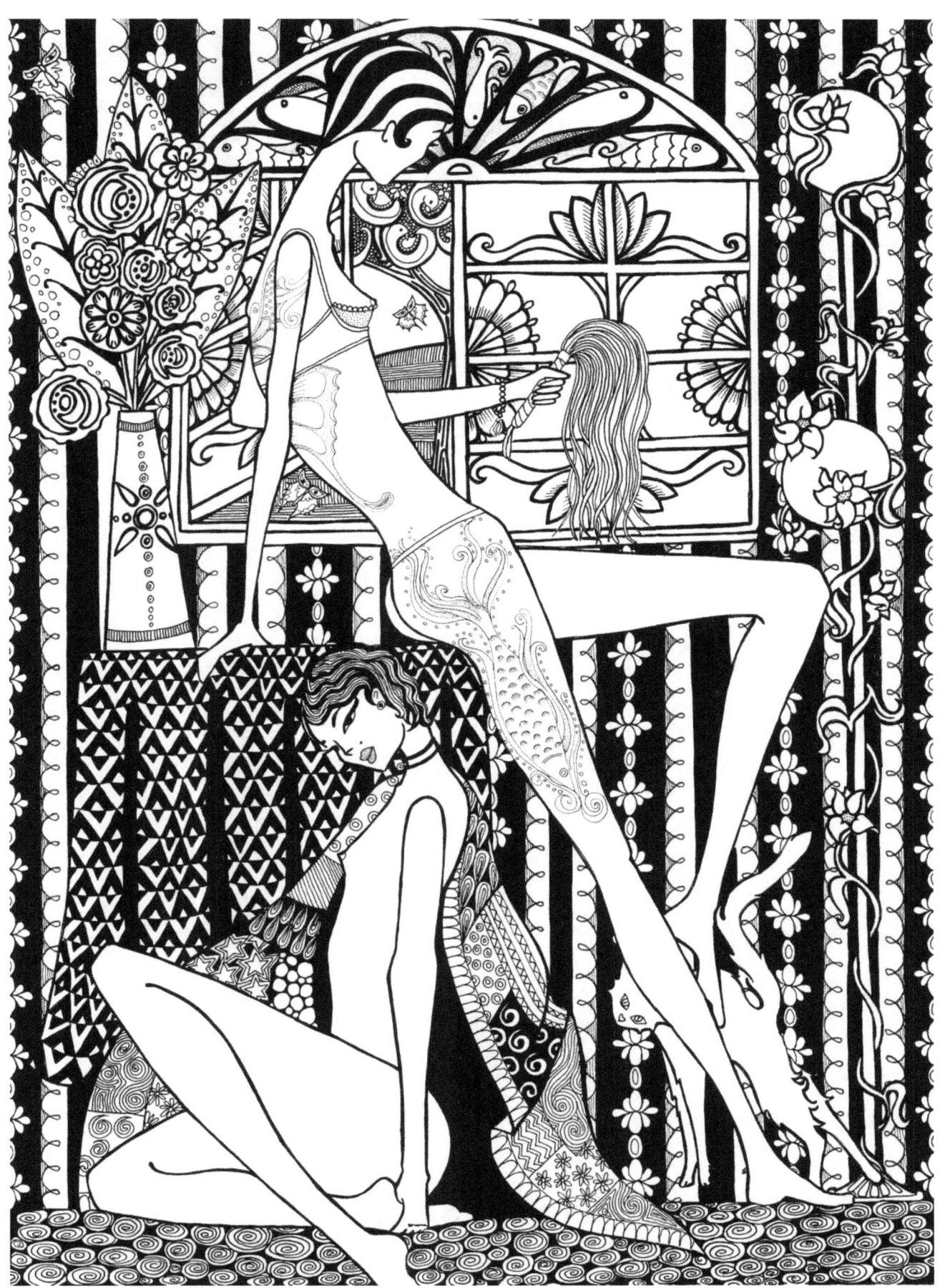

Plate 2 – Siren

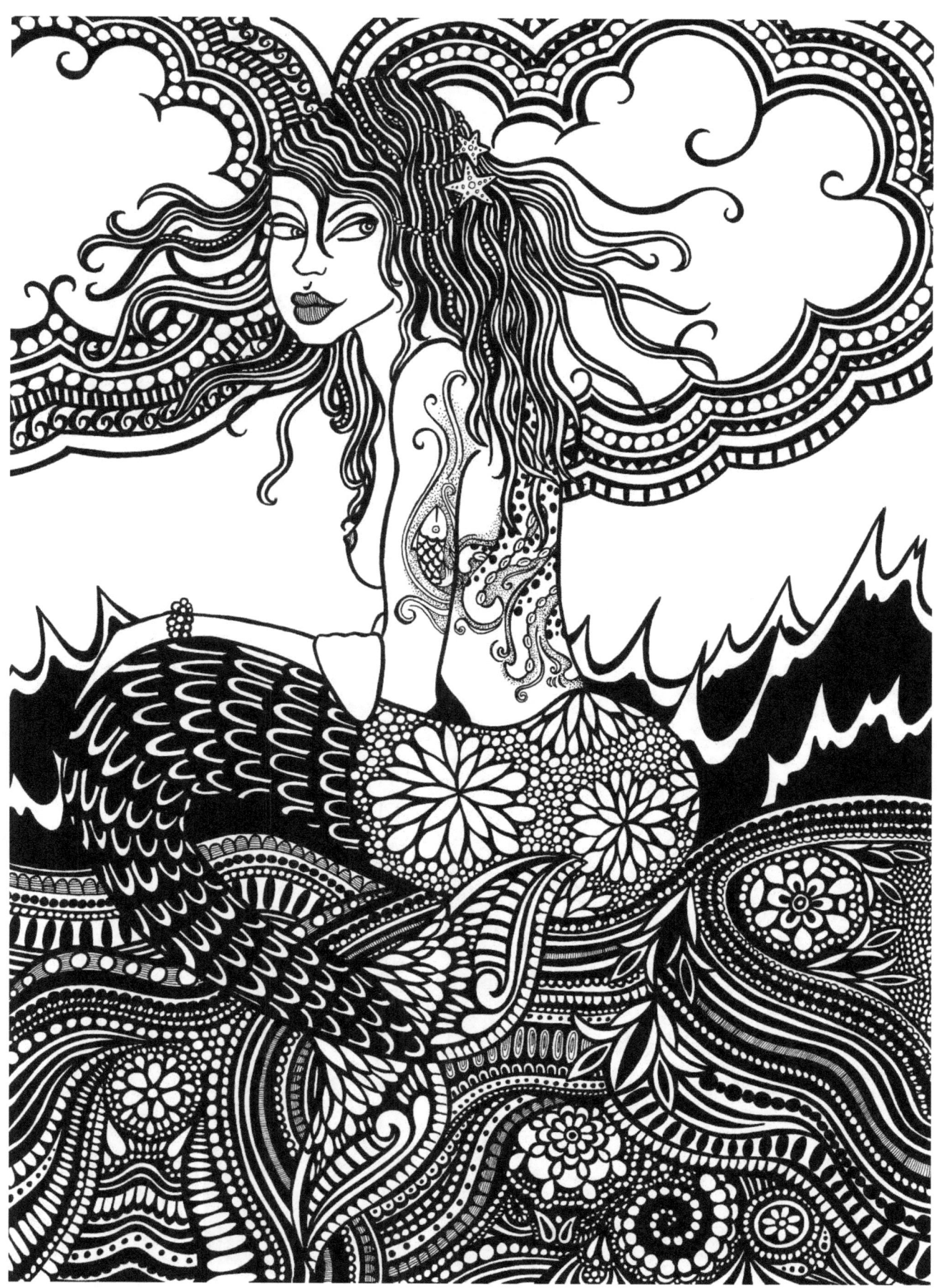

Plate 3 – Cat

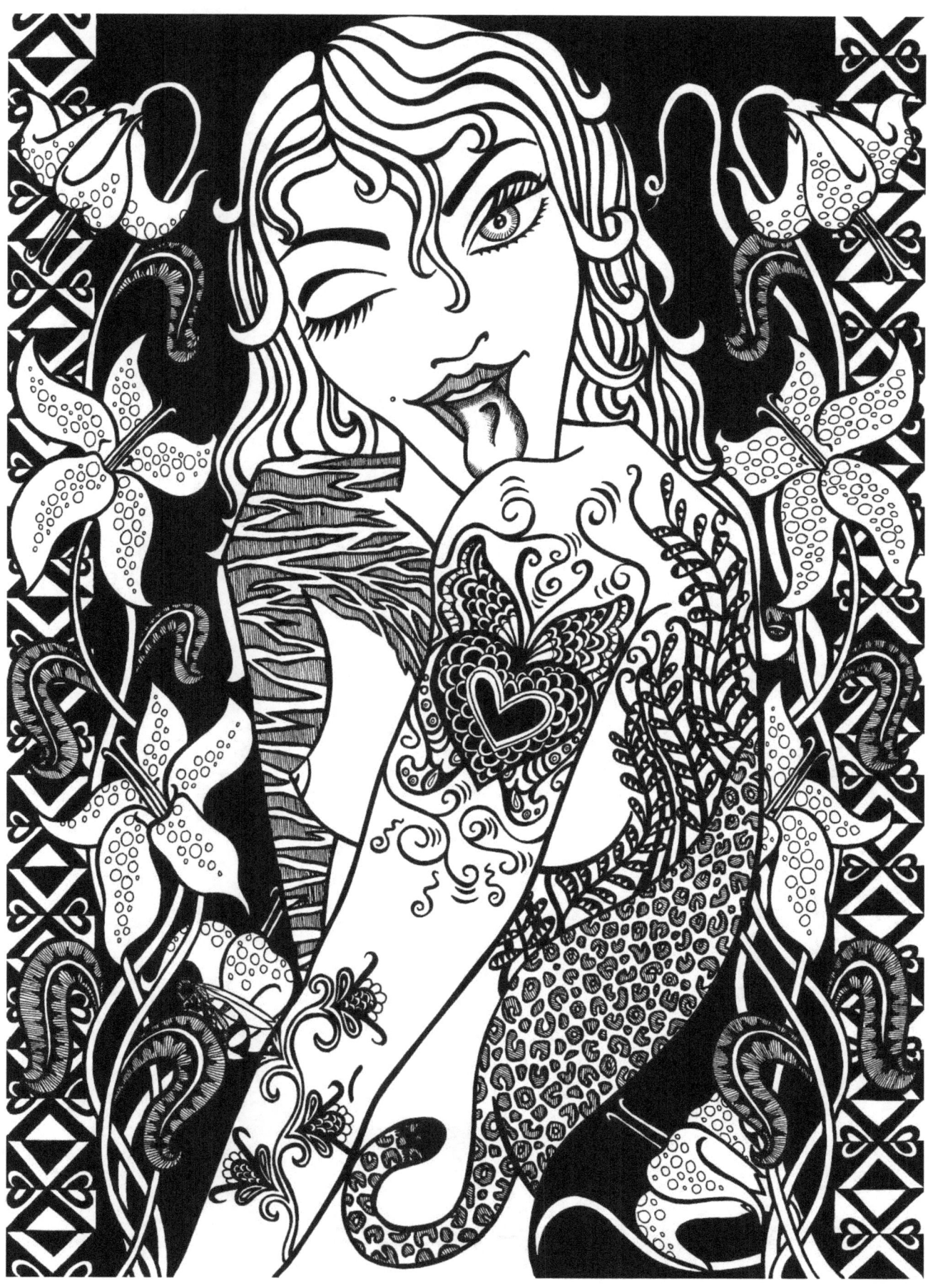

Plate 4 – Ganesha

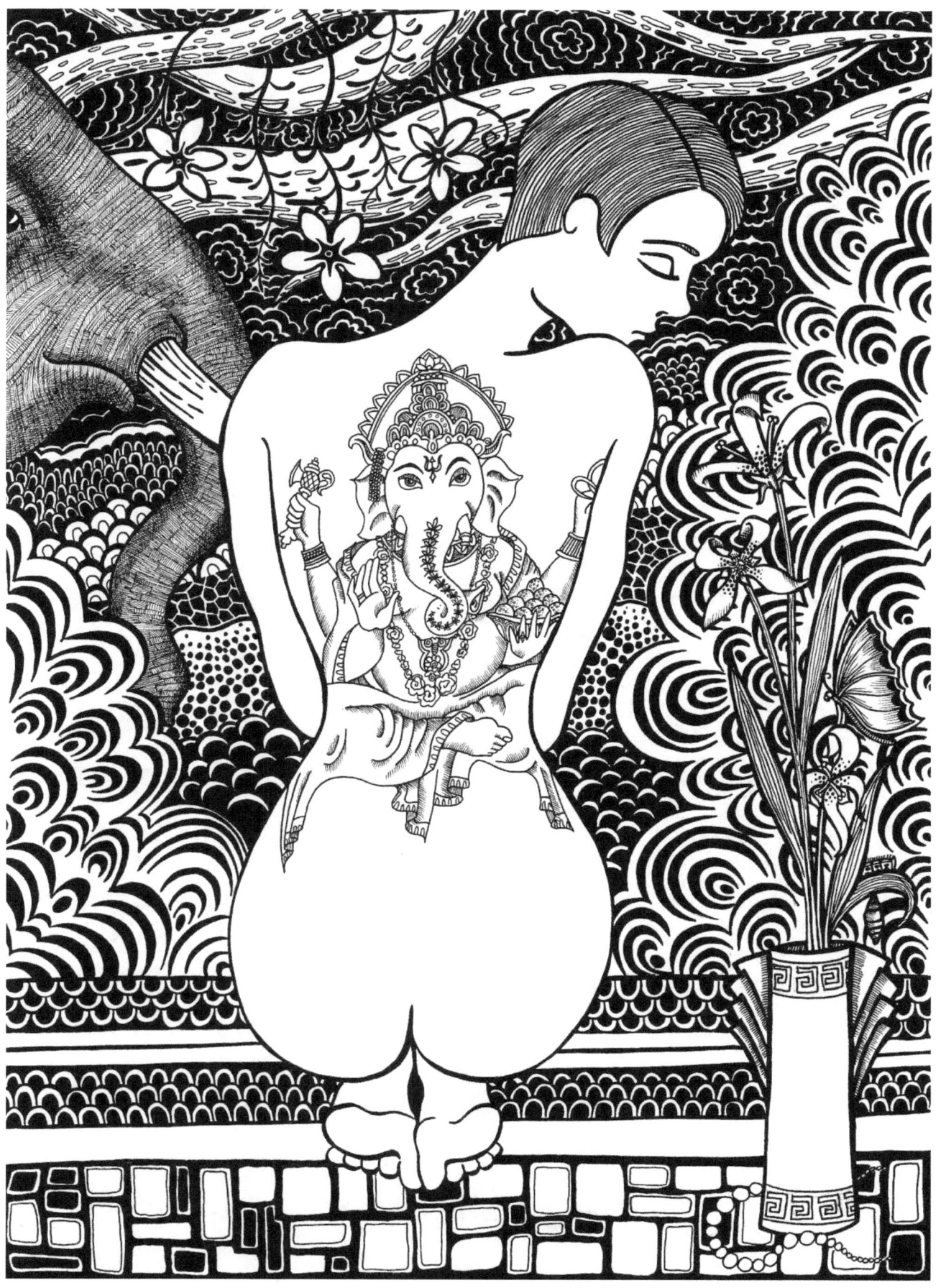

Plate 5 – Listen

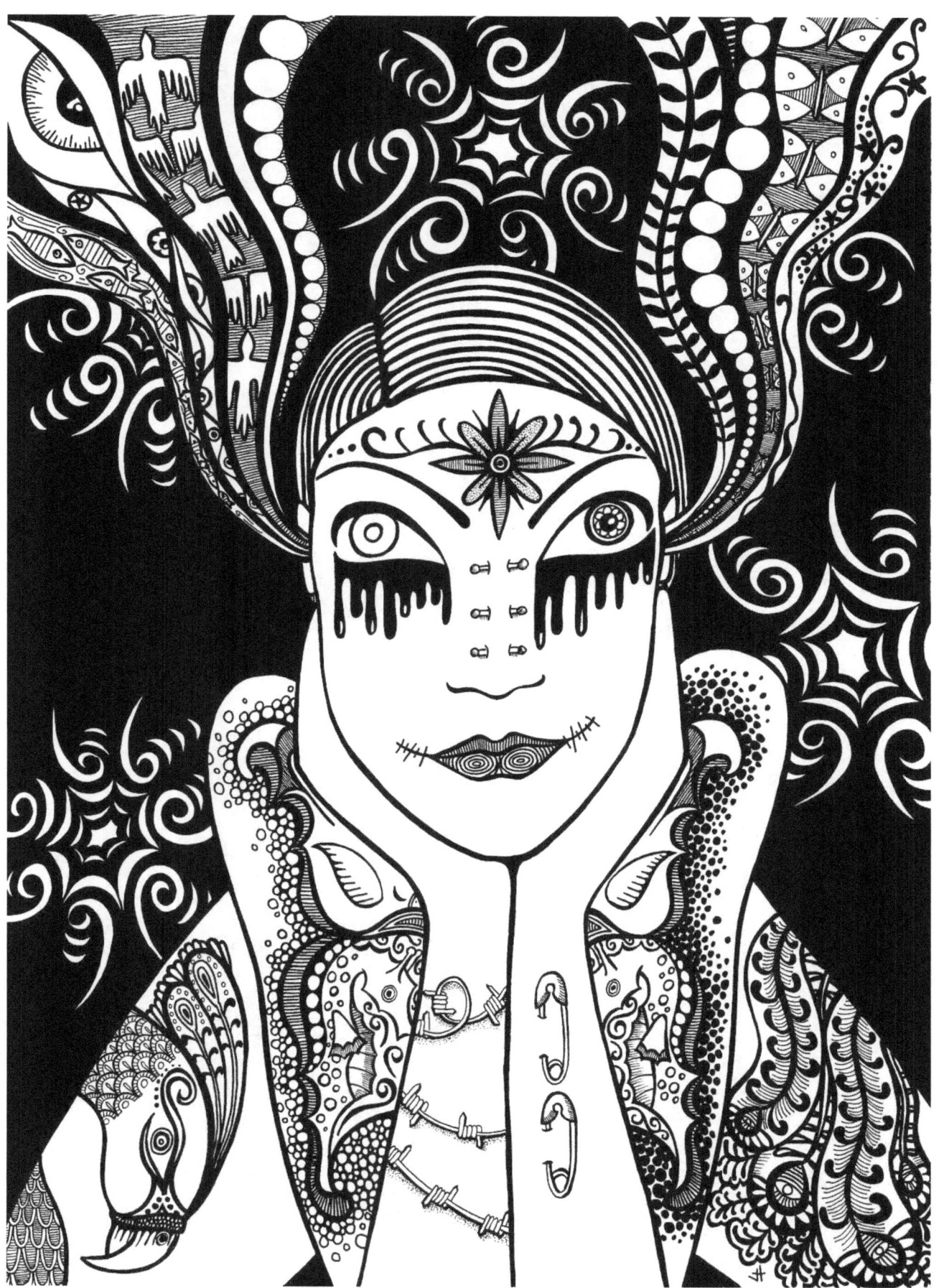

Plate 6 – Ms Andry

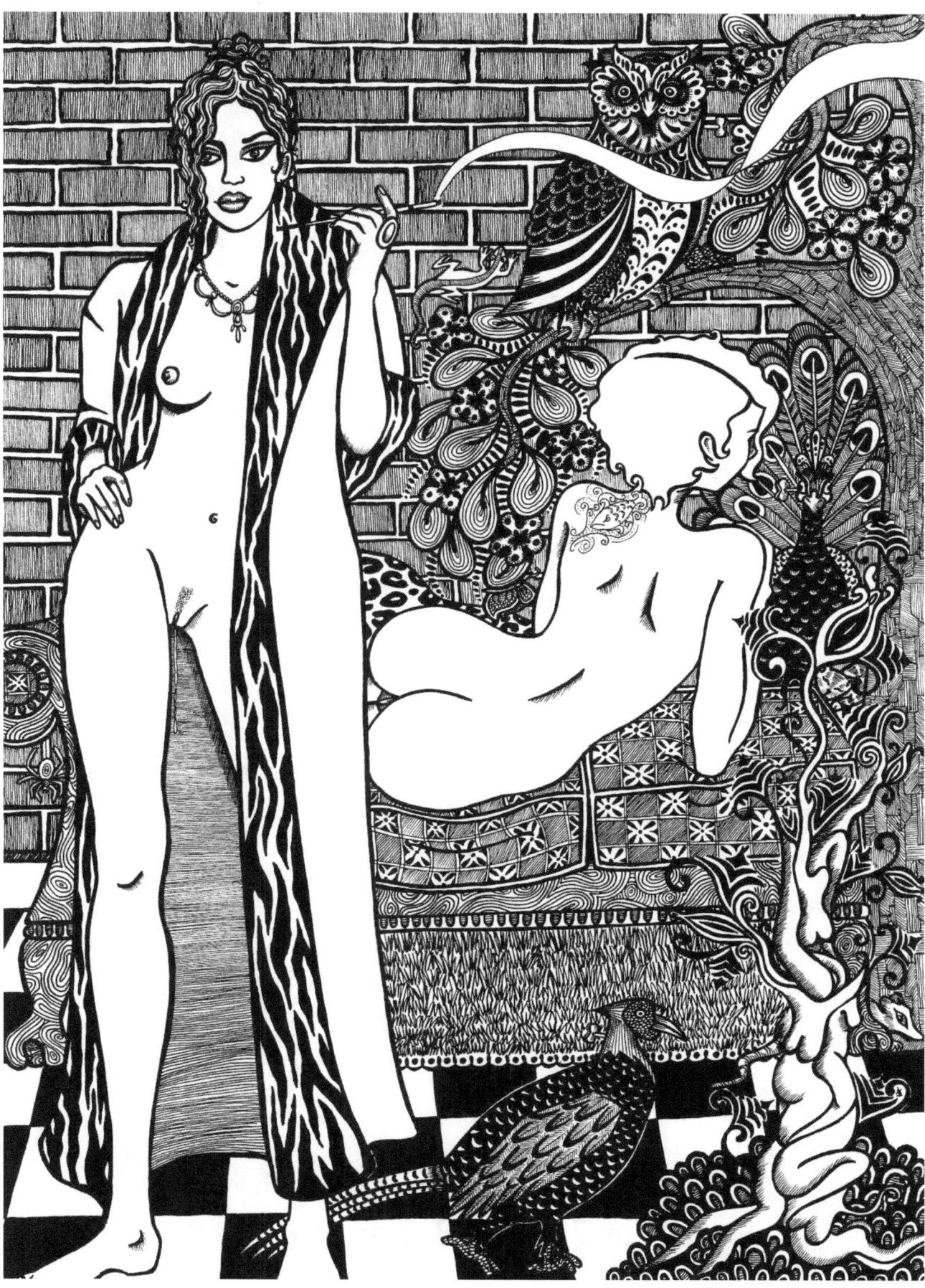

Plate 7 – Ms Behaving

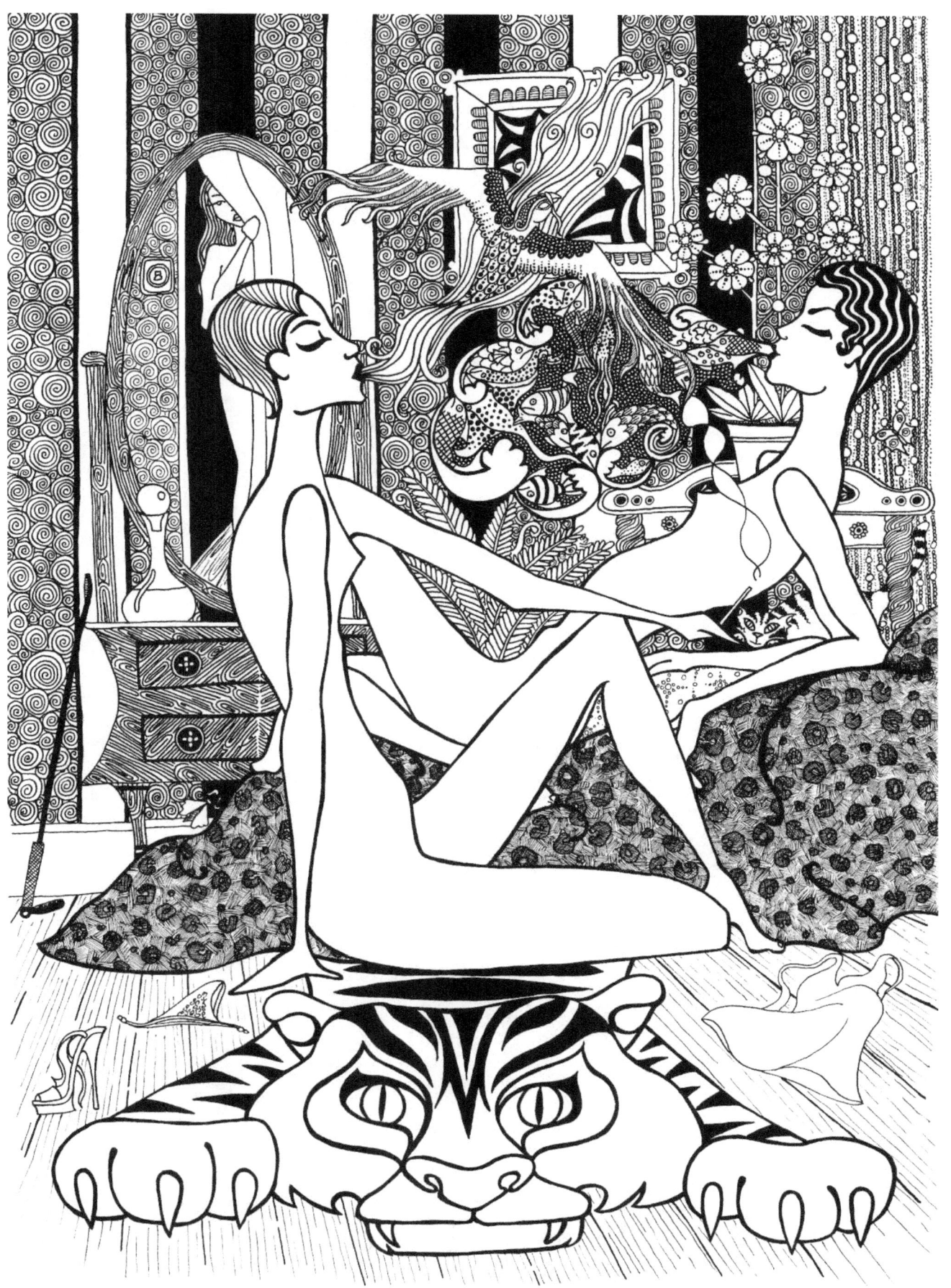

Plate 8 – Punk

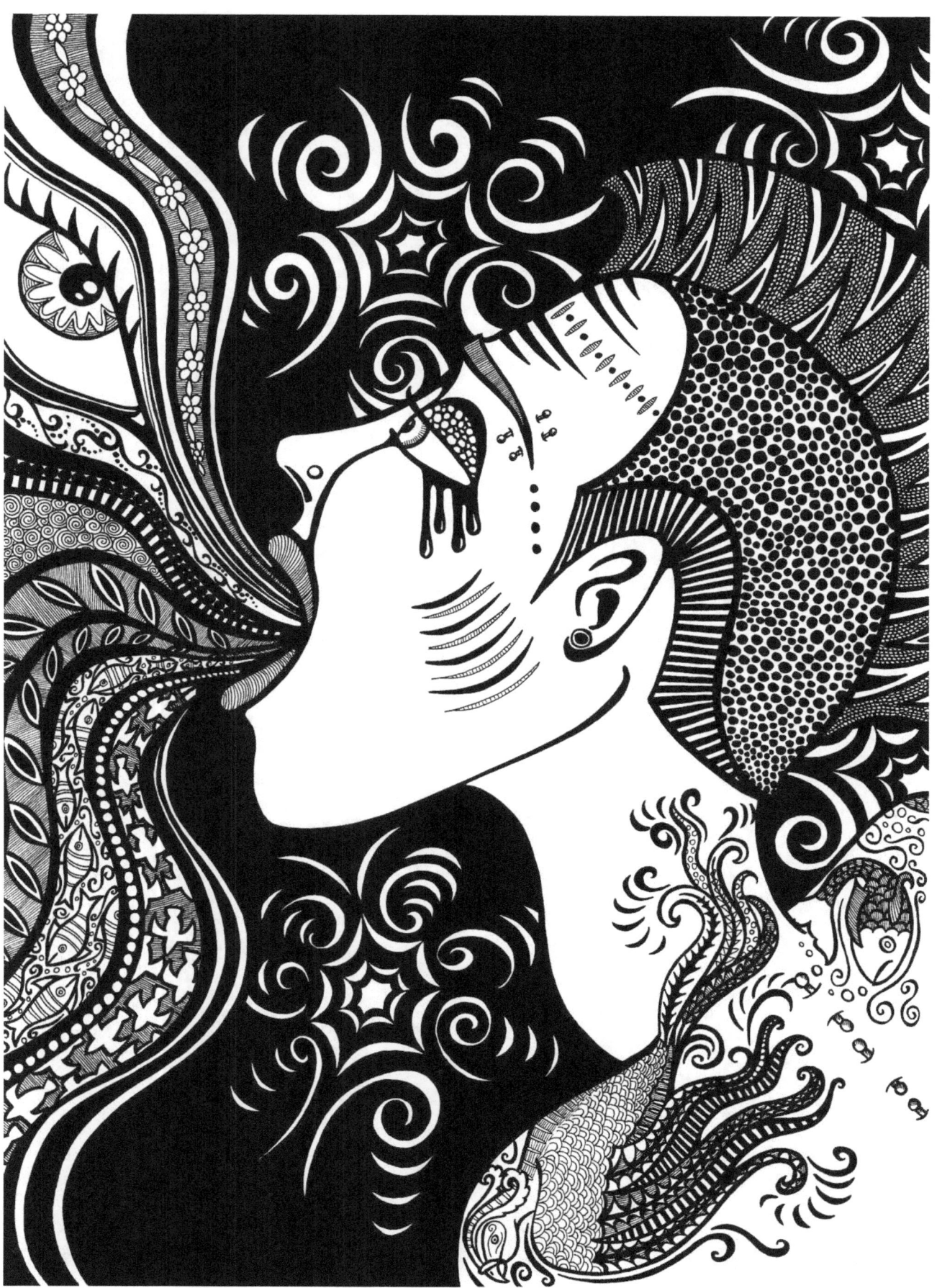

Plate 9 – Tattitude

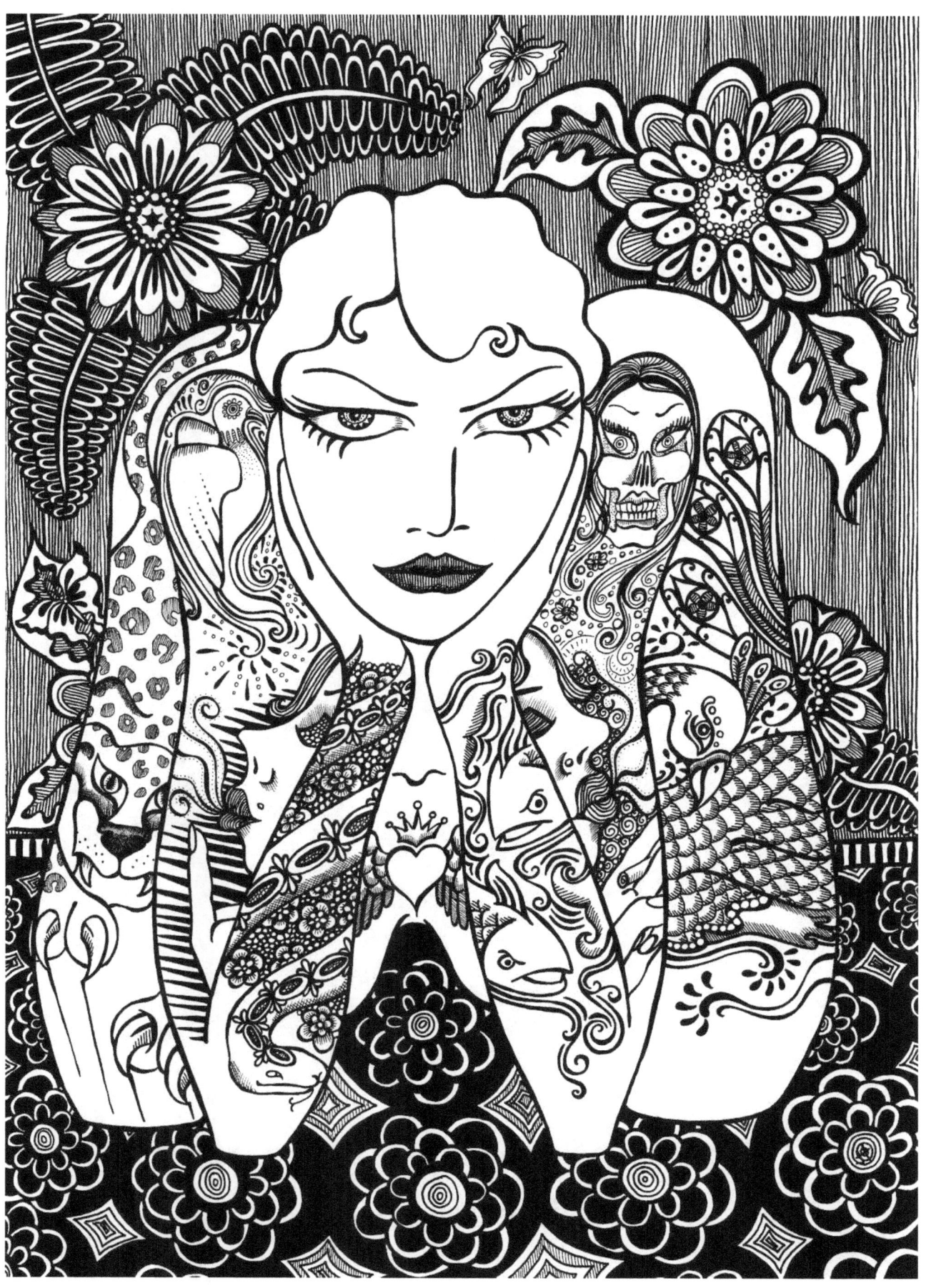

Plate 10 – Miki

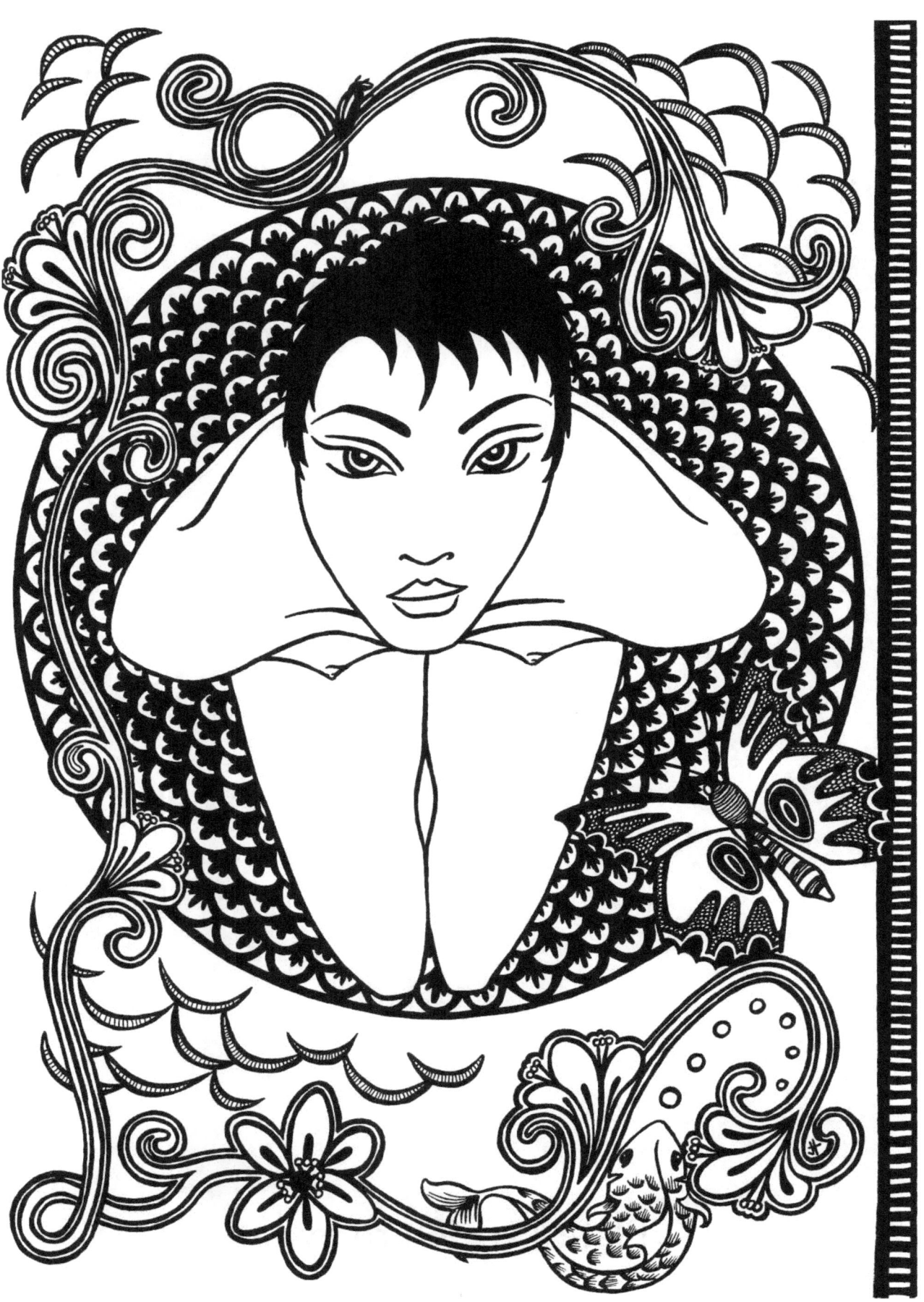

Plate 11 – Third eye

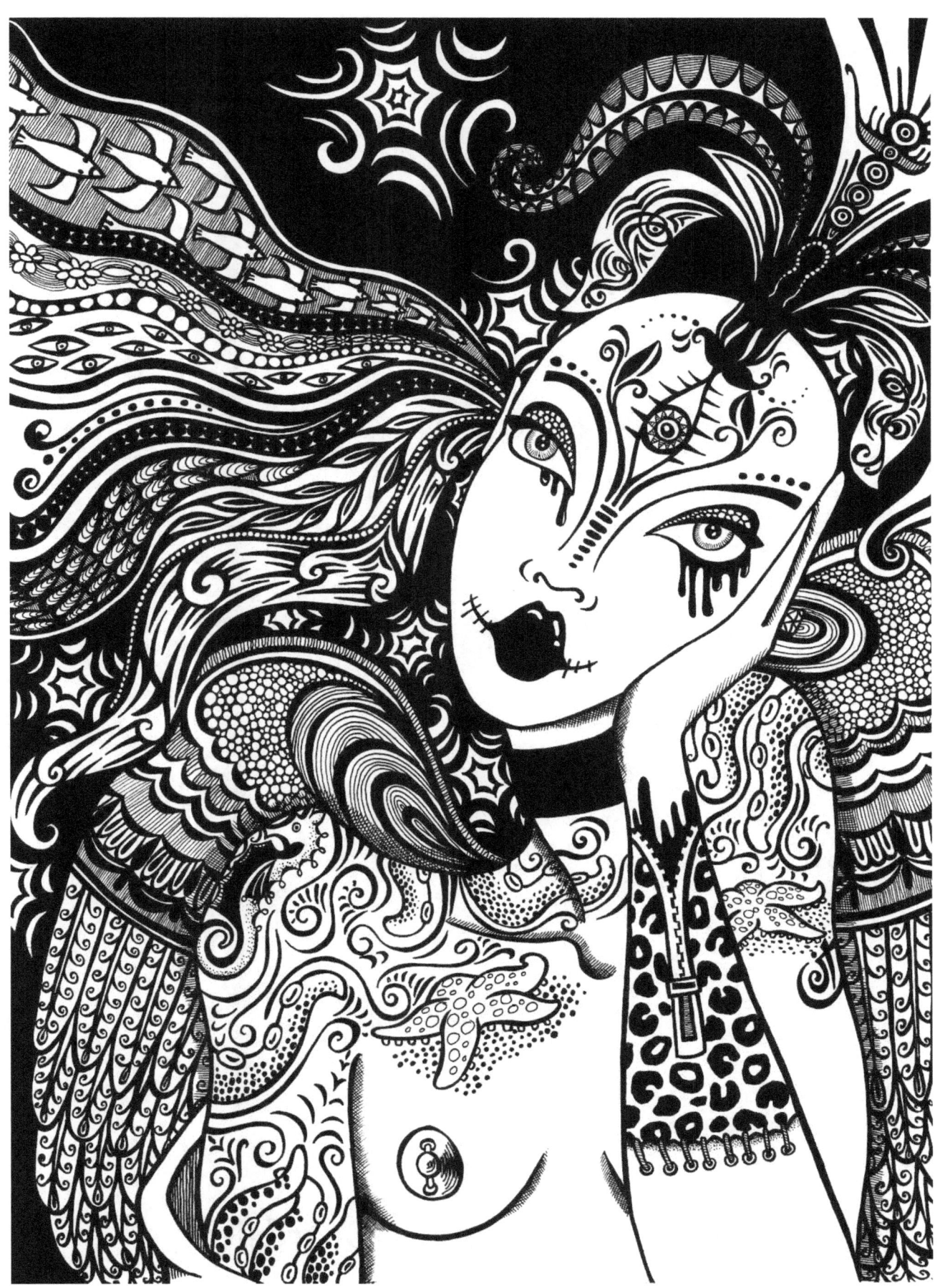

Plate 12 – Dreaming of Beardsley

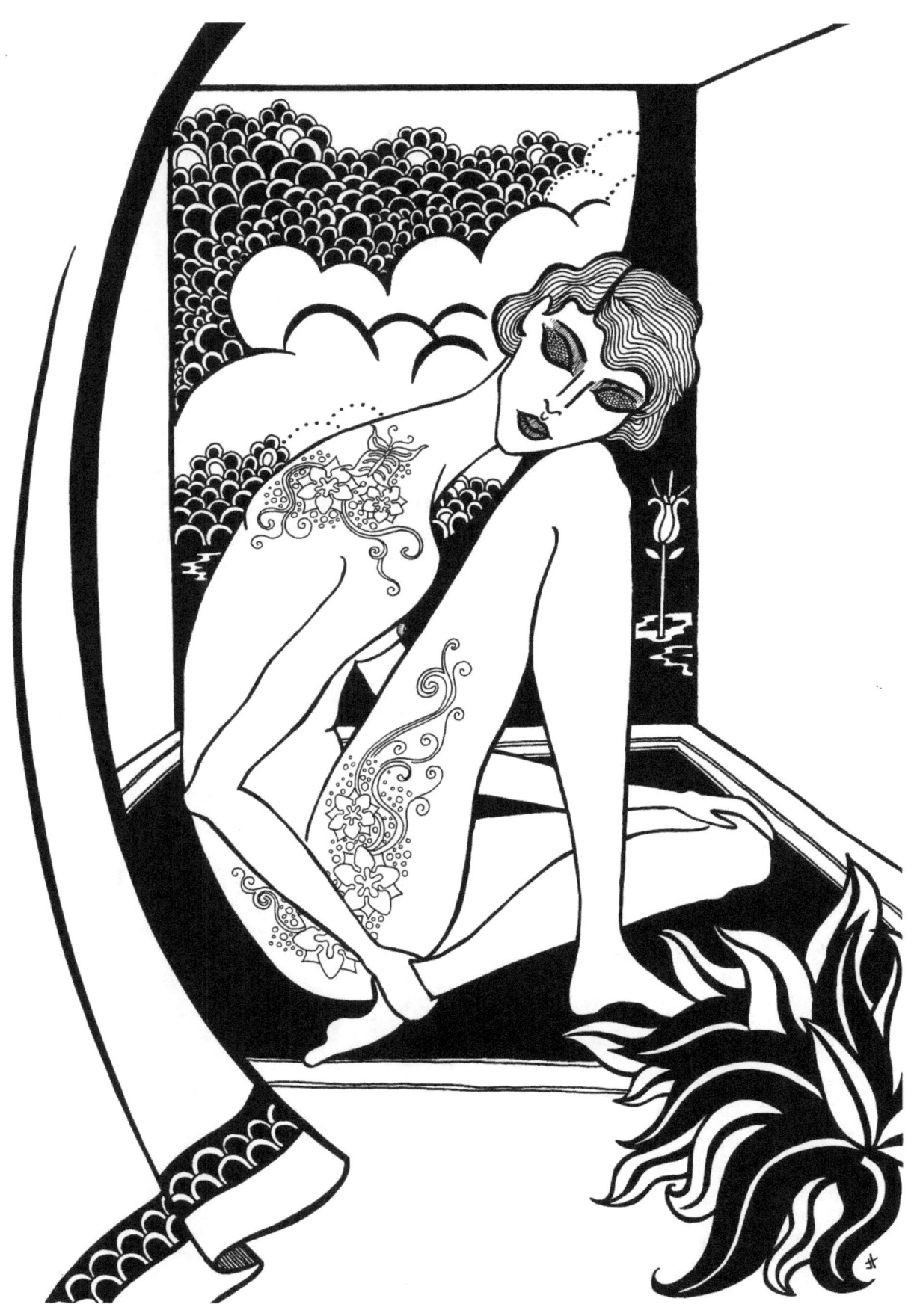

Plate 13 – Ms Conceived

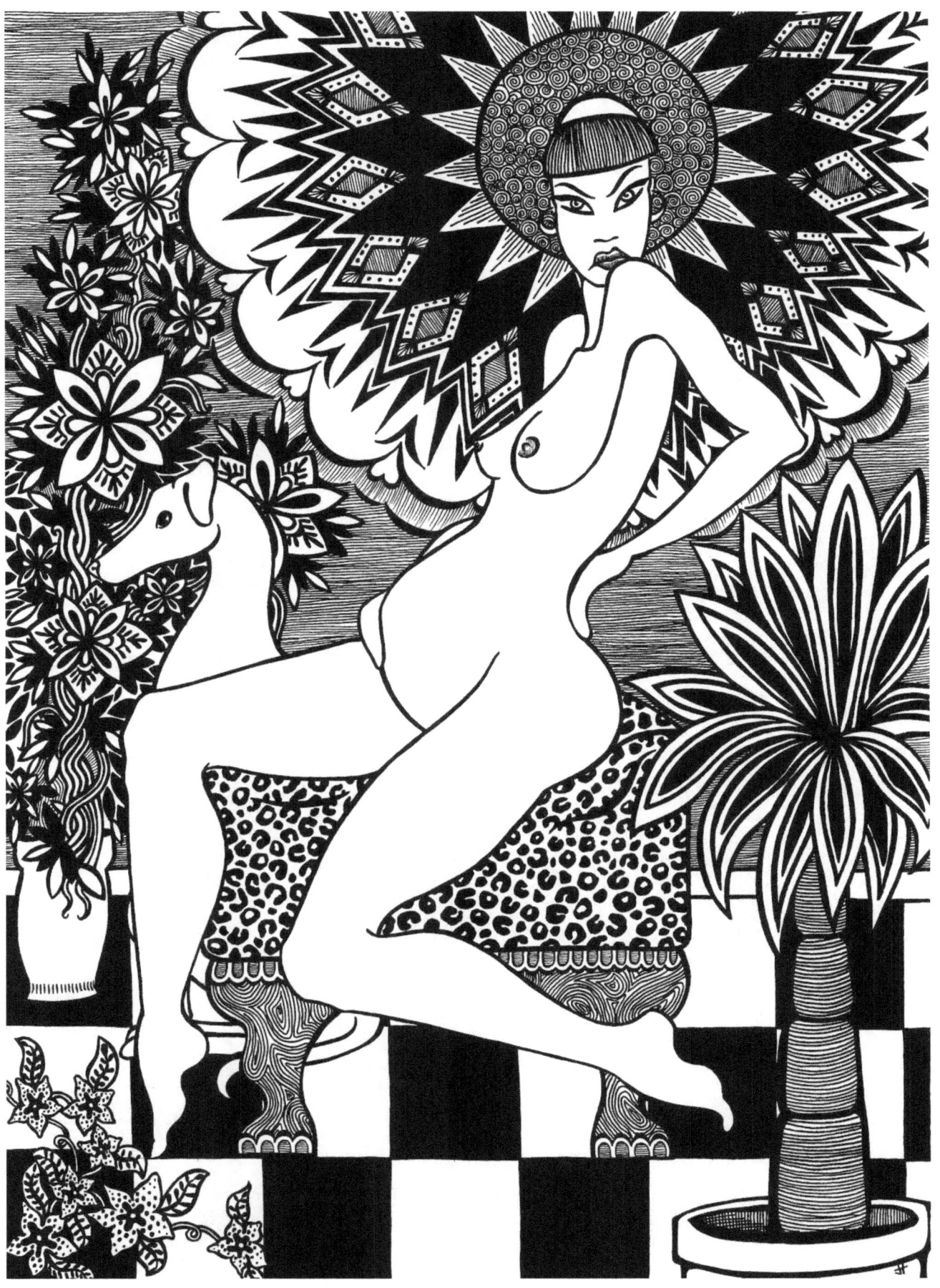

Plate 14 – Ennui

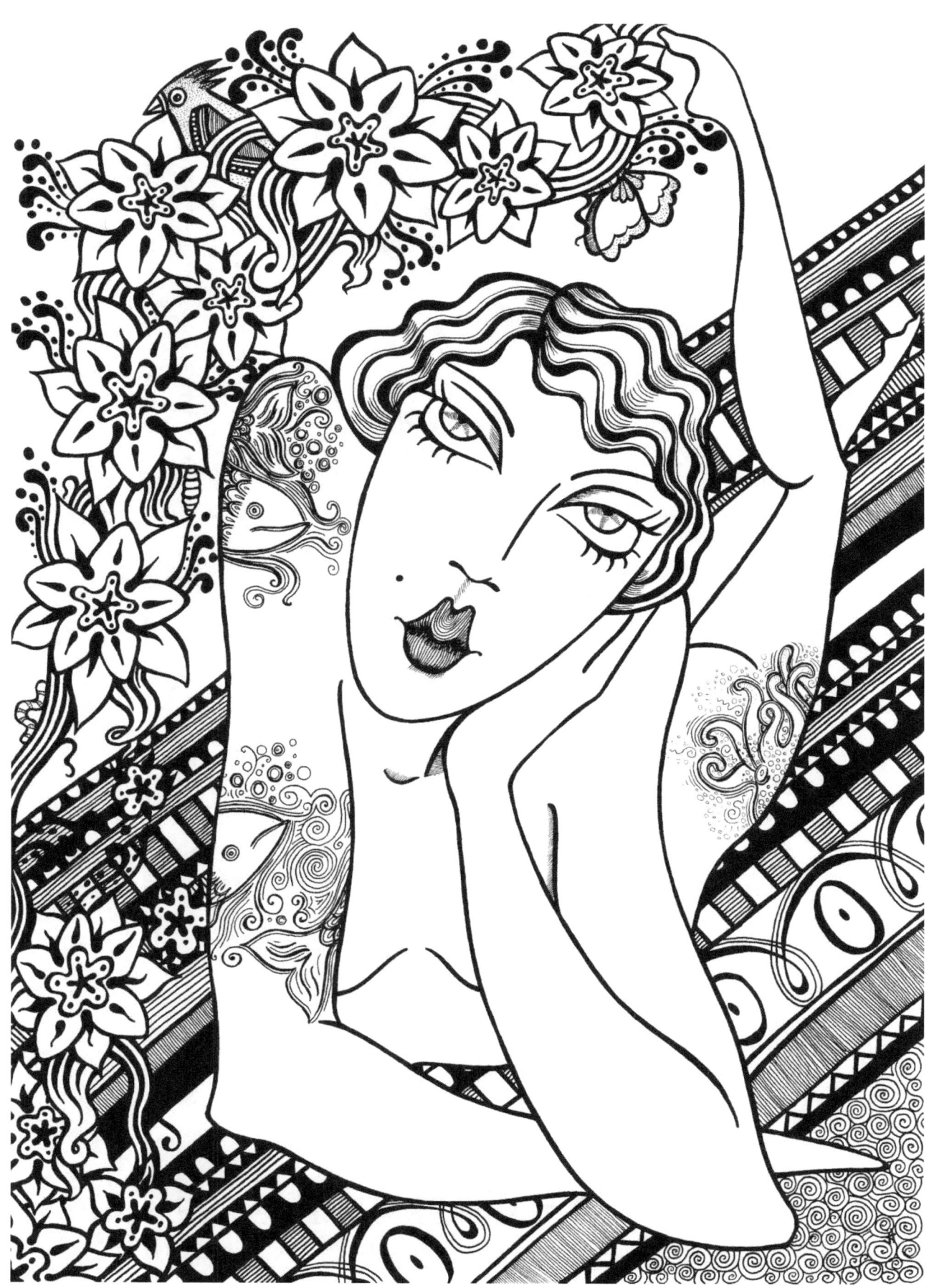

Plate 15 – Wrapped up in you

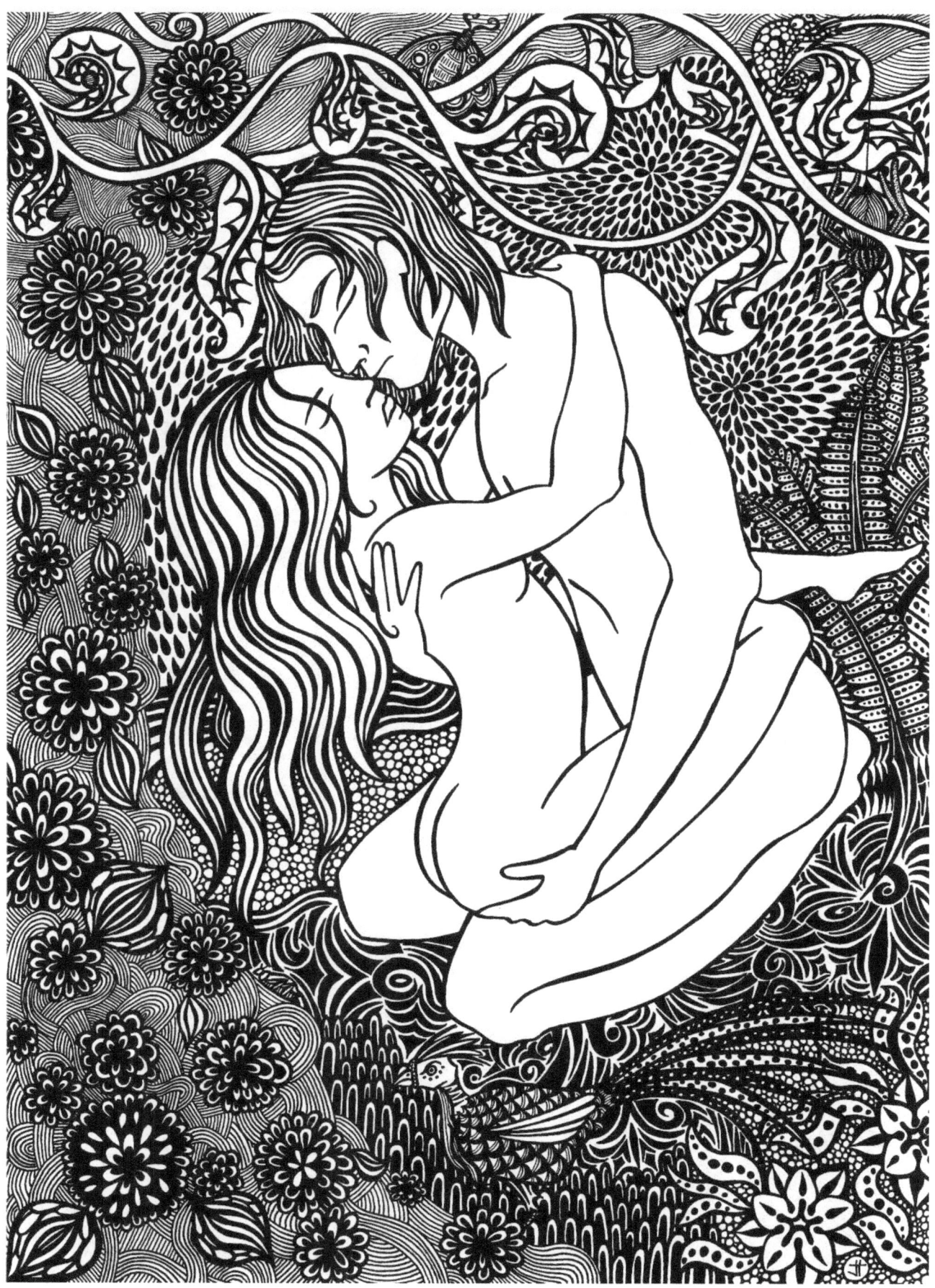

Plate 16 – Daydreamer

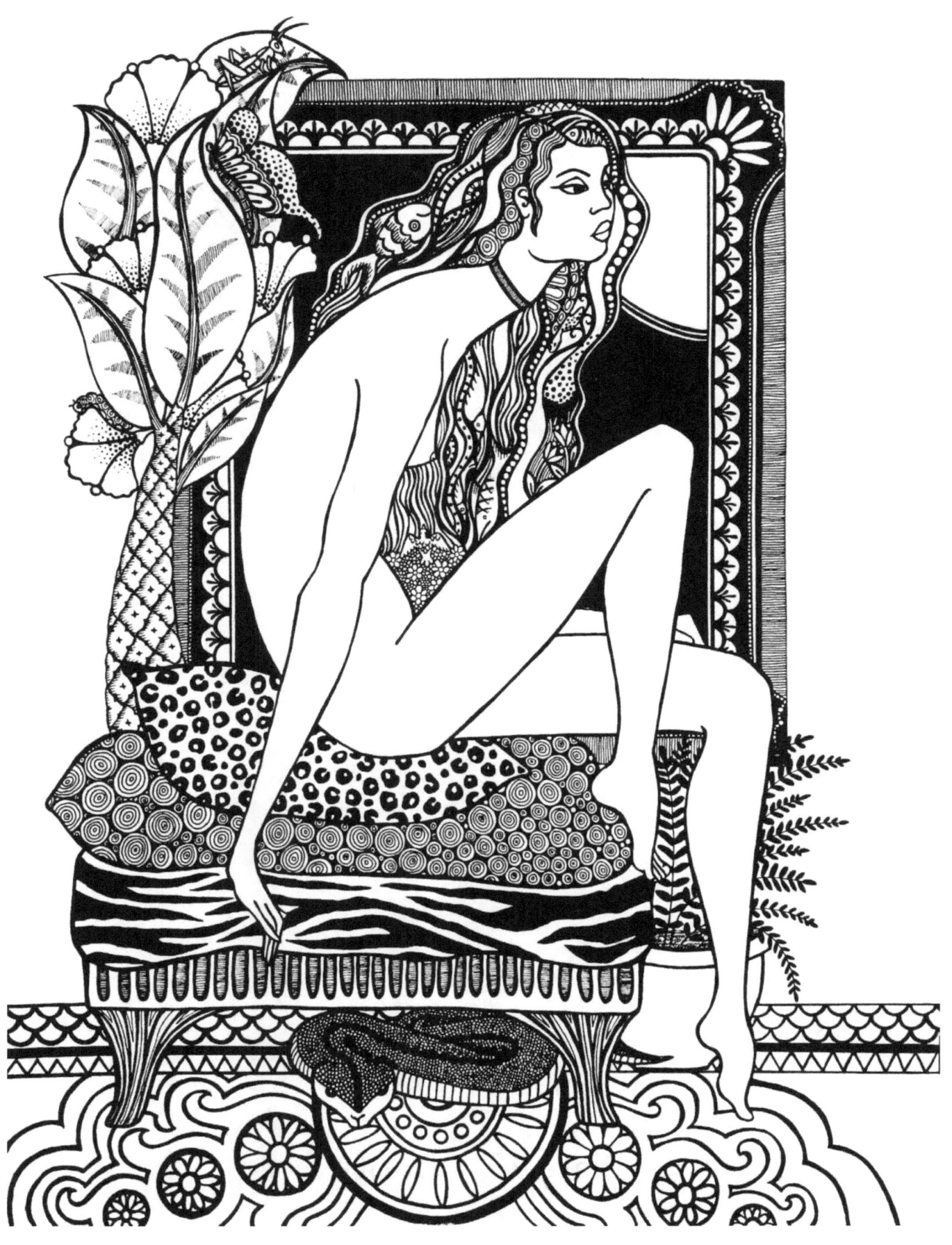

Plate 17 – Booty

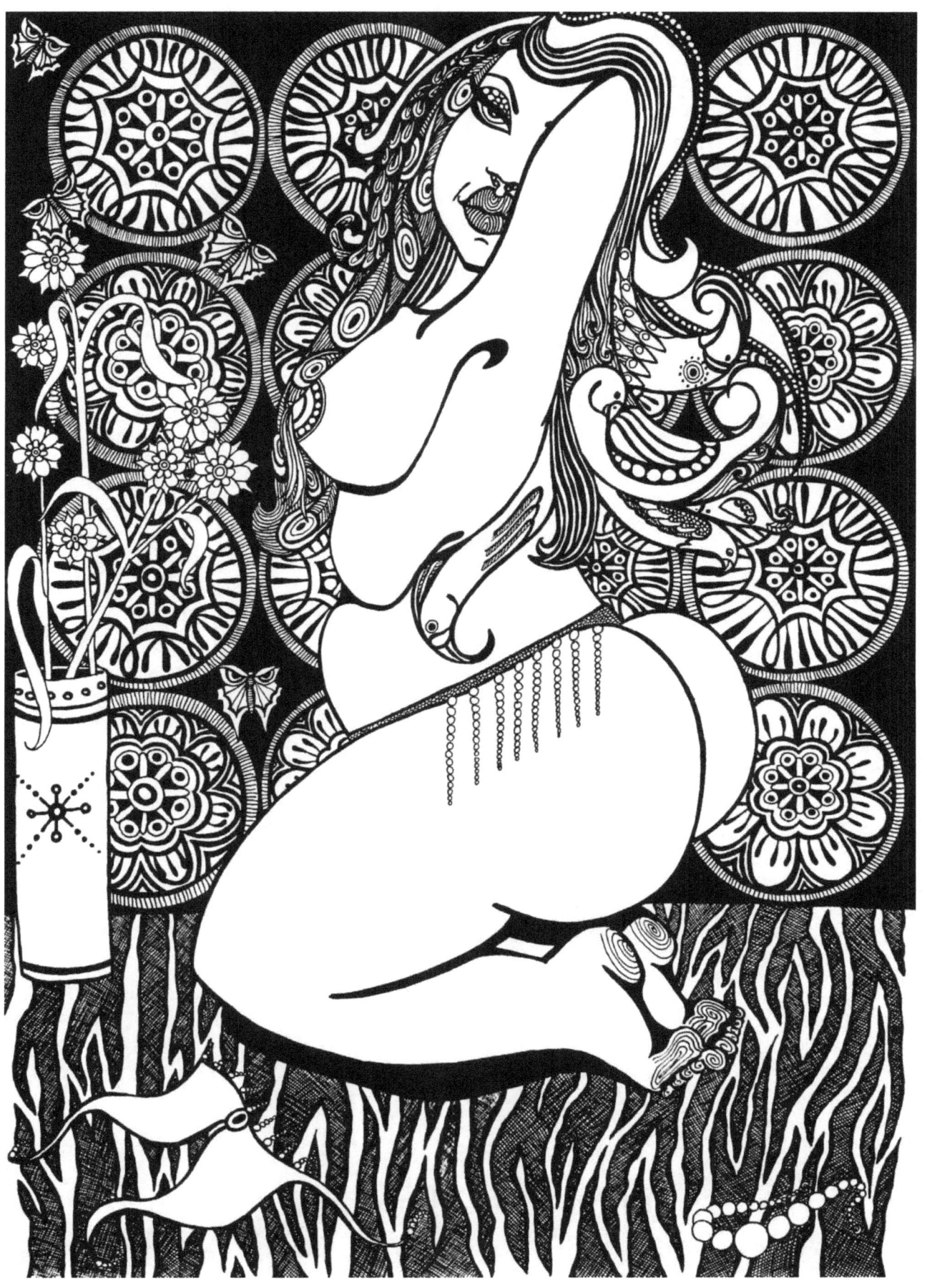

Plate 18 – Flapper

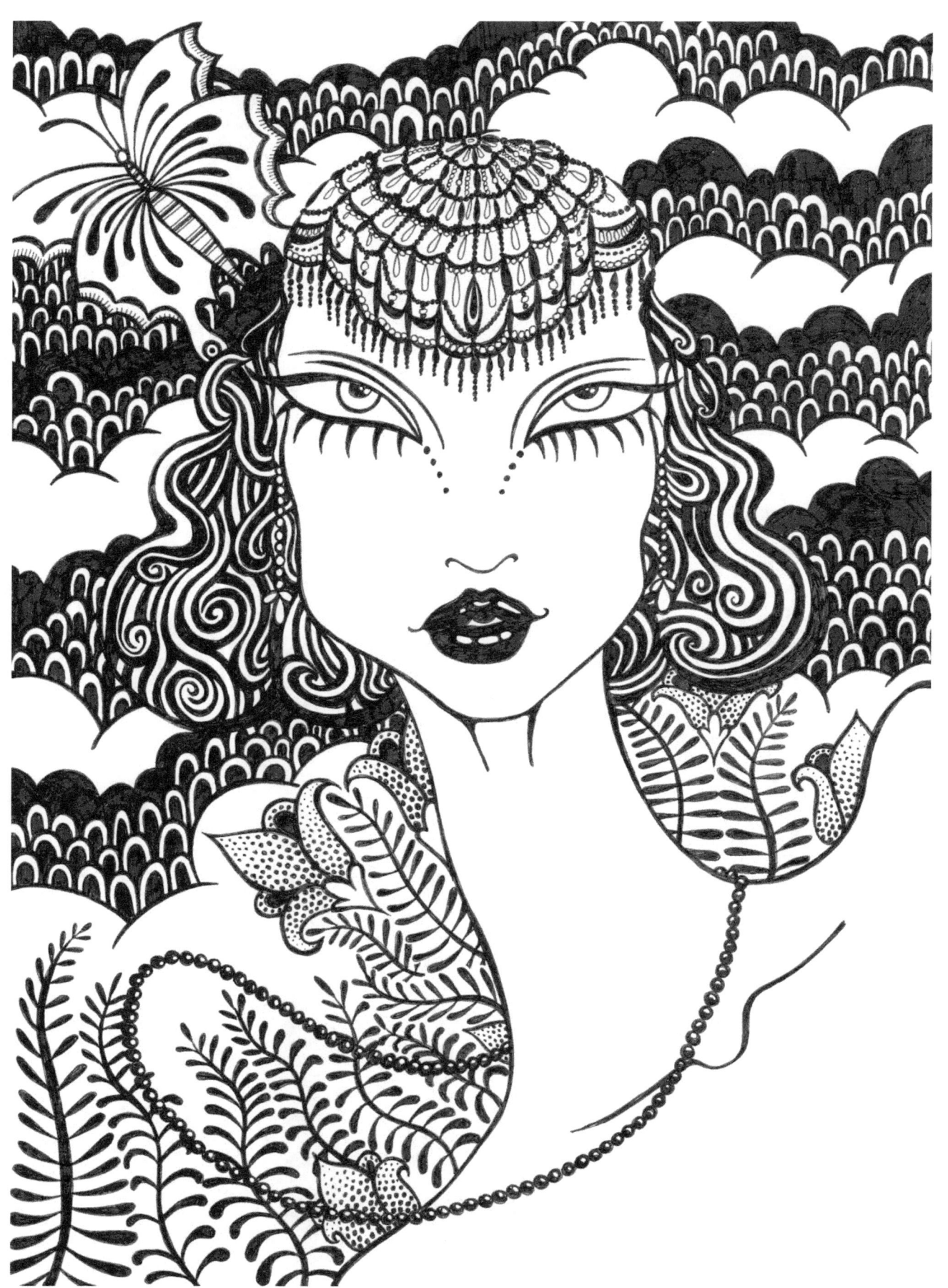

Plate 19 – Lady Garden

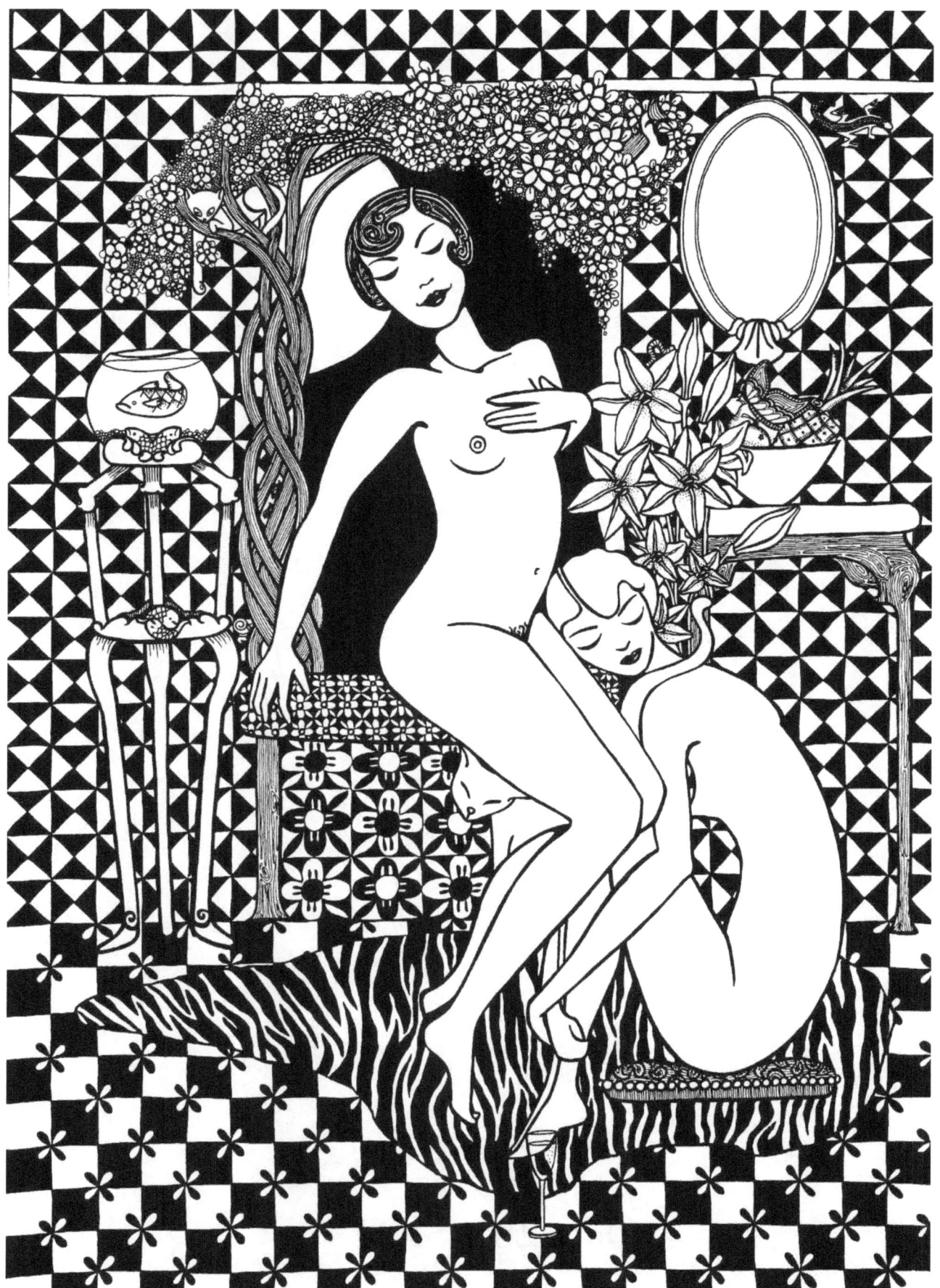

Plate 20 – Shell

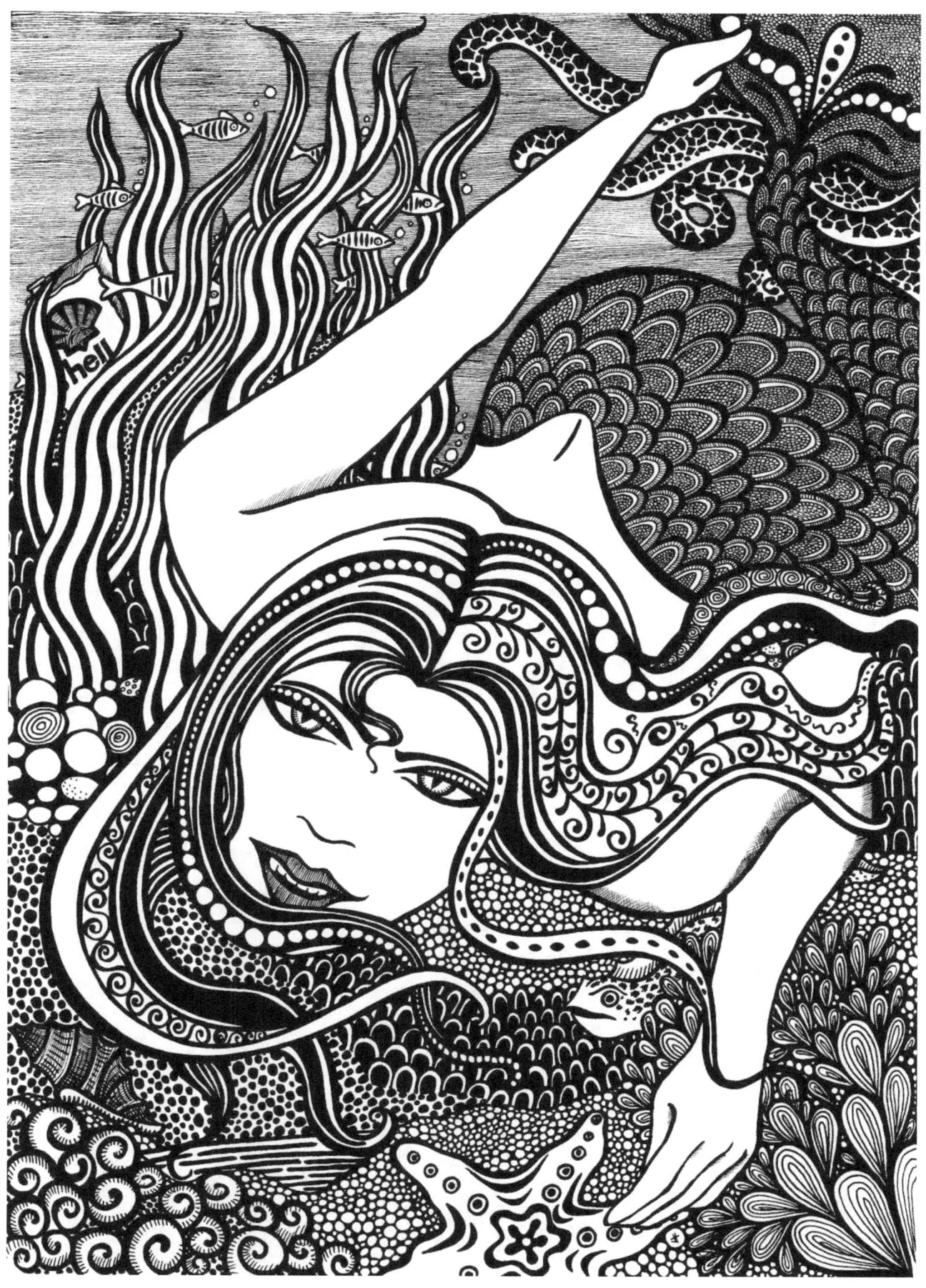

About the artist

Judi Thomas is a human female. This is relevant to her Art. Judi Thomas is her Art. She also makes drawings that investigate, or simply get pissed off with, the male gaze. Not all people with penises have eyes that employ the male gaze. Not all male gazers are men. Not all women have vaginas. Take nothing for granted. Look closely, there is more than you assume, and nothing that asks for your approval. Sometimes her work is about gender politics and sometimes it is simply a celebration of the human form. It is always black and white, but never just black and white.

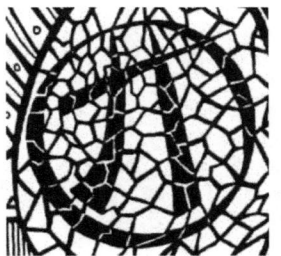

www.ingramcontent.com/pod-product-compliance
Lightning Source LLC
Chambersburg PA
CBHW080614180526
45168CB00007B/2916